Ripple

I0484108

The Ultimate Guide to Understanding Ripple Currency and What You Need to Know

presentation of the information is without contract or any type of guarantee assurance.

The trademarks that are used are without any consent, and the publication of the trademark is without permission or backing by the trademark owner. All trademarks and brands within this book are for clarifying purposes only and are the owned by the owners themselves, not affiliated with this document.

Table Of Contents

Introduction

This short book is for people who are interested in learning more about the Ripple currency and are not sure where to start or what information to rely on. I made this book in response to the high demand of people wanting to know more about Ripple and why there is so much hype around it. The Internet today has a ton of articles and misinformation about Ripple that confuse people who are interested in learning about this revolutionary crypto-currency and possibly interested in purchasing some Ripple themselves.

In this book I am going to give you a short, concise guide for everything you need to know before getting started with Ripple. Understanding the history of this currency, as well as the current innovations that are going on in the Ripple market, are key to predicting what the future will hold. We will also go over the different functions and options that a person has when it comes to purchasing their own Ripple currency and how to use it.

Whether you plan on diversifying from Bitcoin, starting your first crypto-currency with Ripple, or you just want to know more about why this trend is becoming so popular, it is important to know all the benefits and risks involved.

As a side note, I recommend that you take notes while you are reading this book. This will ensure that you get the most out of the information in here. I want you to feel that you made a purchase that is worth your money and so that you can look over the notes of this book even after you've finished reading it. The notes will help you to pinpoint exactly what you need to implement and by writing things down, you will be able to recall specifics and how to handle certain situations when they arise.

Lastly, remember that everything in this book has been compiled through research, my own experiences, as well as the experiences of others, so feel free to question what you have read in this book. I encourage you to do your own research on the things that you want to look deeper into. The more you understand about Ripple, the more educated your decision-making process will be when it comes to purchasing and transacting your own or giving advice to others.

Chapter 1:

What Is A Digital Currency?

When we think of money, we picture it as pieces of paper and round metals that we use for buying merchandise. But throughout the course of history, there have been various forms of currencies over all parts of the world. These have ranged from paper dollars to edibles like salt to round stones that measured 20 feet in diameter (try using that in a convenience store).

The dawn of the digital age ushered in another strange, quirky, and exciting form of money – the digital currencies.

Although there have been digital currencies since the late 90s, things like e-gold and Rand, they were plagued with fraud and hacking, making them insecure and prone to abuse by both the maintaining body and malicious users, ultimately causing their fall. Seeing those flaws and learning from the mistakes of others, math and computer wizards devised a more secure form of currency called the cryptocurrencies. For the sake of simplicity, we'll refer to cryptocurrencies as digital currencies throughout this book.

Digital currencies were born out of the necessity for a monetary form that was not controlled by a central bank and cannot be manipulated by politics or the government. A transaction between two people using digital currency is instantaneous and since there is no central authority, there are no fees or bank accounts needed. Digital currencies were also created because of fear of censorship or having money controlled or confiscated, which is common in unstable countries.

The rules of digital currencies are set by the market, not by the government, so it's free from political interference. This freedom, along with limited supplies, makes it a more stable store of value, at least that's what supporters say. Digital currencies are not affected by inflation or deflation, which can be achieved by controlling the money supply. These features make digital currencies a favorite for libertarians.

Digital currencies, like its conventional counterparts, can be used to buy products and market variables command changes in its value, and is based on some fundamental characteristics of all currencies.

There are currently around 80 different digital currencies available, some created for specific tasks and services. For the purpose of this book, we will be discussing one of the most popular digital currencies in circulation, the Ripple currency.

Chapter 2:

What Is Ripple Currency?

In a nutshell, Ripple is a payment protocol and system that uses XRP, a math based currency. It's a payment system, currency exchange and remittance network built on the same principles of the Internet – free, accessible, and connected. And like many other Internet protocols, no single individual owns Ripple. It allows sending and receiving of money instantly, securely, and nearly free from transaction charges.

Ripple was first implemented by a Canadian web developer named Ryan Fugger in 2005 as a secure payment system for members of a social network through a global network. Currently, it is being developed at Ripple Labs, Inc. and a beta version of the open source has been released to the public in 2013. Being open source, it is free for everyone to use, implement, develop, and modify. And no one profits directly from   its   use.

The Ripple Protocol and Network

Unlike physical and virtual financial transactions which are controlled by organizations, Ripple transactions are controlled by the Ripple protocol and can be used for virtually any type of transaction that can be translated into monetary value.

Running on a network of computer servers around the world, the Ripple protocol uses mathematical algorithms in verifying the accuracy of financial transactions. Ripple is based on a publicly shared ledger, a constantly updated database of Ripple accounts and transactions, and anyone can view the ledger and see all records in the Ripple network.

XRP: The Ripple Currency

The XRP exists only within the Ripple system and is the native currency of the Ripple Network. It was designed to be secure, fast, and direct.

It is based on complex and powerful mathematical algorithms, following fixed rules that cannot be changed. Every transaction in the Ripple network consumes a small amount of XRP which is equivalent to, at most, a few pennies, even in high-volume transactions. This security cost feature protects the system from abusive users who try to spam with massive amounts of transactions because they will run out of XRP during the process and will be forced to stop. XRP can't be duplicated, falsified or even created.

XRP transactions are processed by a global network of distributed servers which run the Ripple protocol, working seamlessly with the Internet, making it a very fast way to transact.

Payments using XRP are direct and peer-to-peer without the need for intermediaries, third-parties, or other institutions. In the physical world, it is like paying directly with cash because there are no delays in processing, chargebacks or frozen accounts. There are also no transaction, network, or operator costs, except for the tiny security costs mentioned above.

The smallest unit of XRP is called a drop, and 1 million drops is equivalent to 1 XRP, making it mathematically divisible by 6. There's a finite number of XRP created – 100 billion, and no more can be created according to the rules of the Ripple protocol. Unlike traditional currencies, which can be produced by the government as needed, XRP was designed to be a scarce asset, and its supply decreases as it is used. 20 billion XRPs have been retained by the creators of Ripple and the rest is gifted to Ripple Labs for distribution.

Like other currencies, XRP has a value that is affected by market changes and fluctuates against the dollar, yen, euros, and even another digital currency, Bitcoin. This makes XRP ideal as a bridge currency, facilitating exchange between two currencies when there is no direct exchange available, like what happens when transacting between two rarely traded currencies.

XRP is not affected by inflation because the number of XRP never increases. Inflation usually happens when more money is produced, making it less valuable as a whole. Just like gold, which has a finite amount and with increasing scarcity, you can decide how rare, how useful, and how valuable it is.

By the way, XRP is also called Ripple in layman's term for simplicity. We'll be using the terms interchangeably in this book.

Gateways and Pathways

Gateways are individuals or organizations that allow users to move money in and out of the Ripple network. In a nutshell, gateways facilitate deposits and withdrawals. They can be similar to banks, but only share one central ledger, which is the Ripple network.

If you need to deposit $500 into your Ripple account, the gateway you selected will transfer the amount into the Ripple Network after you have sent the amount via your local bank. The gateway will facilitate the withdrawal through a method or service it offers like bank transfers, check or cash.

Pathways are links between users, institutions, and gateways. An example of a traditional transaction flowing in pathway links is when an American customer buys a product in China using his Visa credit card via PayPal. The payment transfer goes through his local bank who issued the credit card, to Visa, to PayPal, and then to the local bank of the vendor.

Although the online purchase only takes a few minutes, the actual transaction only completes after verifications from each of the links and can take 2-5 business days before the merchant actually receives the payment in his/her own bank account, with each institution adding fees for the use of its service. Needless to say, it is relatively slow, expensive, and restrictive.

Ripple pathways are designed to be open, faster, and easier to use. Since only you can control your account without any intermediary institutions involved, it cannot be frozen and there are no terms of use applied to it. No penalties, limits, or prerequisites.

RTXP – The Ripple Transaction Protocol

The Ripple Transaction Protocol or RTXP follows the principles of other Internet protocols like HTTP for the World Wide Web and SMTP for emails. Like the Ripple currency, the Ripple, it is controlled by mathematical principles through the use of complex algorithms.

RTXP runs on computers around the world and maintains a perfect shared record of transactions, accounts, and balances in a distributed database called the ledger. RTXP continually and automatically updates this database and it is replicated to thousands of servers around the world, so there's no single point of failure. The update within the database happens in a few seconds, just like the time it takes to complete a transaction in the Ripple network. RTXP also dictates that no more than 100 billion Ripples will be available, so it is not susceptible to inflation.

For any currency, payment system security should be of utmost importance and RTXP makes sure that the Ripple network is reliable and safe. All accounts and transactions are encrypted and algorithmically verified. Only account holders can authorize payments and no one has special access to the network, while the distributed nature of the system provides no single point of failure or attack.

Ripple is free for everyone to use, develop, and/or modify. Programmers can download the Application Programming Interface or API kit from the Github repository without fees, signups, or approvals. They can start developing new real-money applications or integrate Ripple into their software in order to provide additional financial services. Additionally, users can access their Ripple accounts using open-source software called the Ripple Client.

Chapter 3:

What Are the Advantages of Ripple?

Fast

Riding on the power of the Internet and a network of servers configured for distributed computing, Ripple transactions are comparably fast. While normal bank to bank transactions take 2-5 business days, Ripple payments are cleared in a matter of seconds, even if the transaction must be done halfway around the world. The network of servers running the RTXP protocol comes to consensus on the state of the ledger, payments are processed, balances are adjusted, transactions are executed, trades are completed, and the process begins again, all in a few seconds time.

Distributed FX

Currency exchange is one of Ripple's most important features giving the users access to a global currency market. It effortlessly enables cross-currency payments using Ripple as a bridge currency. Trades are processed without the intervention of brokers, intermediaries, and other middlemen, so there are no fees incurred.

It is the only currency exchange and the first one in the world that allows trading in all currencies or any unit that has value like frequent flyer miles, virtual currencies, and mobile minutes. The system selects the best available exchange orders and processes the exchange automatically. Cross currency payments allow sending a payment in dollars from the United States and arriving as yen in Japan, or Yuan in China, using the best available exchange rates without margins or fees.

Secure

Using advanced cryptography and complex mathematical algorithms in verifying accounts and transactions makes Ripple very secure. Only the account holder can authorize the payment and since there are no third party institutions in the middle, there are no counter-party risks.

Like paying cash, Ripple payments are irreversible. Hosted in a global network of servers around the world, the Ripple system has no single point of failure or attack, making it safe from hackers and other malicious users.

Cheap

The only cost incurred on Ripple transactions are what is called security cost, and is an essential part in securing the system. Other traditional payment systems charge an amount that is controlled by for-profit organizations for the use of their services in making payments. The Ripple payment network can be used by anyone, is owned by no one, and is controlled by the Internet – which is a free for all protocol.

This also means higher profit margins for merchants because of the elimination of fees charged by banks and other financial institutions acting as intermediaries during the transaction. Merchants get the full payment because receiving payments in Ripple is free. Micro-payments in Ripple also allow payments of any size, even a tenth of a penny, which can then allow the creation of new business models and pricing systems.

Chapter 4:

How Do I Use Ripple?

Now that you know what Ripple is and how it can benefit you in your financial transactions, how can you begin to use it?

Creating a Ripple wallet

To get started using Ripple currency, you need to open a Ripple wallet using the Ripple Client available by typing the URL: https://Ripple.com/client/#/register in your browser. You just need to fill in the username and pass-phrase you want to use to create your own Ripple wallet. You will then be presented with a Ripple address and a secret account key, which you can use in case you forget your account details or passphrase.

Activating your Ripple wallet

Now that you have your Ripple wallet, you need to activate it before you can use it for funding your account with other currencies, trading, sending, and receiving. This is a protection for automatic account creation, which can be used by malicious users. You need to transfer a minimal number of XRP (currently 20) into your account and there are several ways to do this:

You can ask someone who already has an activated and funded Ripple account to give or lend you the required number of Ripple.

Some of the available gateways will automatically activate your wallet when you transfer funds to them.

Bitcoins can be also be purchased and converted into XRP, which can in turn be used to activate your account.

You can participate in Ripple Labs giveaways to get free XRP. One giveaway asks you to donate your idle computing power to scientific research and is open to personal computers and Android devices.

You can join the Pay it Forward (PIF) initiative by Ripple Labs. You will be asked for the minimum number of Ripples you need to activate your account and if you are lucky or convincing enough, you might just get it. But you are expected to do the same to others making the same request.

Choosing a Ripple Gateway

As mentioned earlier, you need a Ripple Gateway before you can start transacting in the Ripple network. Once you sign up with one, you can begin to use Ripple's powerful features like payments, distributed currency exchange, and others.

Choose your gateway according to the following guidelines:

Is it reliable? - You will need to do a little research and investigation on the gateways available and choose which one you trust the most.

What are the currencies available? – Which currencies do you usually transact with? These will be your preferred currencies. Select a gateway that allows for these currencies.

What are the available deposit and withdrawal methods? – Gateways offer different deposit and withdrawal methods such as bank transfer, check, or cash. Choose one that suits your preference.

What are the fees charged? – Some Ripple gateways may charge certain service fees. Have them explain clearly their fee structures and select one that fits your needs.

Although Ripple Labs is not affiliated with any gateway, they prefer ones that are members of the International Ripple Business Association. Currently, these include Snapswap, Bitstamp, RippleCN, The Rock Trading, RippleChina, and Justcoin. The IRBA was formed to provide procedures and policies in establishing secure services for Ripple users.

Signing up at gateways is simple and straightforward. Just visit the site of your chosen gateway and provide some basic information like your name, email address, and Ripple Wallet Address. Most gateways will need to verify your email address to prevent fraudulent accounts from being created so you will need to provide a valid email address that you have access to.

How to Fund Your Gateway Account and Send Money to Your Ripple Wallet

To fund your gateway account, you will need to provide bank account details, like account number and routing number, so that online transfers from your bank to the gateway can be facilitated.

Once you have setup your gateway, you can then send money to your Ripple wallet by following these steps:

Type in https://Ripple.com/client/#/login into your browser. Enter your username and passphrase.

At the upper tabs, click on Advanced, then the Trust tab on the left side of the page.

Setup a trust limit with the gateway for an amount equal to what you want to send to your wallet. If you deposit $500 at Bitstamp and you want that amount transferred to your Ripple wallet, a trust line that amounts to at least $500 should be created first. This sets up the trust on your Gateway, making it possible to send funds to your Ripple Wallet's address.

Log in to your gateway using your user ID and password for their site.

Go the withdrawal page and choose Ripple payment as the transaction method.

Put in your Ripple wallet address as the destination of the transfer.

Put in the amount you want to transfer and the currency.

You can now transfer money from your gateway to your Ripple wallet.

Here are the steps on how to do it the other way around and transfer money from your Ripple wallet for withdrawal:

Log in to your gateway's website using your ID and password.

Go to the deposit section and choose Ripple deposit.

Enter the specific Ripple address that is connected to both your gateway and your Ripple account.

After the money arrives in your gateway account, you can withdraw the money through any method supported by your gateway, like over the counter withdrawals, check, or bank to bank transfer.

How to Trade Using Ripple

Ripple was the world's first distributed currency exchange system. You can freely trade with different currencies without requiring the services of brokers, and other third party institutions. You just submit the buy or sell prices to the Ripple network and it will automatically find the best available match and complete the trading process for you. Here is a step-by-step guide:

Log in to your Ripple wallet account using your username and passphrase.

Click on the Advanced Tab on the upper part of the main page.

Click on the Trade tab located on the left.

Manually enter a currency pair or select one from the drop-down list.

To select an issuer for both currencies, click 'Change Issuer'. You don't have to do this if you are trading XRP, since it does not require an issuer. Issuers are gateways that allow withdrawal of funds from the Ripple network. One example is Bitstamp.

Enter the Public Address of the issuer and click Confirm.

To check the current trading trend for the currency pair you selected, look at the Bid, Ask, Spread and Last price values. For example, if you want to trade dollars for yen, check the offers to buy and sell dollars for yen.

If you want to see a more detailed view of open currency offers, you can also click 'Order Book'. You will see the best ask and bid values displayed at the top.

Choose Buy or Sell, select a price and amount, then click 'Place Order'

Check the trade values and click Confirm to submit the trade offer. A message will first appear that says your trade request has been submitted, and then another one that says your request has been accepted.

Check the Wallet Activity List for the status details of the order. You will see your account balances being updated accordingly so you might see only partially filled orders as the trade progresses. If you have outstanding offers, they will remain open if they are completed or if you have opted to cancel them.

Chapter 5:

The Future of Ripple

Compared to traditional currencies, Ripple is still quite new and the global financial industry is just starting to embrace it. It's still in Beta as of this writing (January 2014) and the currency exchange feature is only available to users with XRP reserves and active accounts. Of the 100 billion available XRP, around 7 billion has been distributed, still a long way to go before the supply is depleted. Experts predict that the value of Ripple will start to go up when all XRP is in the hands of the public.

Of the 80 billion gifted to Ripple Labs, a large part of it is being used and will continue to be used for charity donations. Their giveaways are already helping science and medical research through donating processing power in exchange for XRP. Ripple Labs is expected to have more of these projects in the future.

Bridge protocols are additions to the RTXP protocol that allow payments to external networks. Ripple payments can be sent to Bitcoin addresses because of the Bitcoin Bridge protocol. Bridge protocols for email, SMS, and bank accounts are still being developed. The goal is to allow Ripple payments to be sent to any kind of account.

Ripple and Gateways are some of the latest evolutions in the financial industry and with them, payments and trades are faster and cheaper. This could open new financial opportunities to both vendors and customers.

Being third to Bitcoin and Litecoin as the most popular digital currency in circulation, Ripple is being compared to silver by market analysts, while Bitcoin is gold. They've based it on the value, rarity and available supply, or the scarcity of both currencies. They can see Ripple as the last payment system we'll ever need and use for it as a payment network as well as a trading platform.

It should be noted that Ripple might never approach the value of Bitcoin. The main reason is that Bitcoin is much rarer than Ripple. Only 21 million Bitcoins will be created compared to Ripple, which has a supply of 100 billion Ripples. There are almost 5,000 times as many Ripples as there are Bitcoins. And just like precious metals, the rarer it is, the more valuable it becomes.

The 100 billion Ripples should have a total worth of 80 trillion USD to match Bitcoin at its current market price. The current value of Ripple is 0.0185 USD while Bitcoin is pegged at 838 USD. We're using the Bitcoin-Ripple comparison because these are two of the three most stable digital currencies in the world right now.

Using the values above, and Winklevoss's prediction that a Bitcoin could cap at 33,000 USD in the future, we're looking at a peak value of 0.94 USD for a Ripple. And some experts are predicting that Bitcoin could cost more than 100,000 USD per piece. A conservative, more realistic, near-future prediction puts 10,000 USD per piece of Bitcoin and 0.29 USD per Ripple.

...But Ripple is not just a currency

Ripple is not just a currency but it is also a payment and distributed exchange network. This increases the viability of Ripple more than Bitcoin. If Bitcoin, Ripple, and other digital currencies collapse, the Ripple network might still be there if financial institutions and the general public accept it.

Based on the security and reliability features of Ripple, according to experts, the future looks bright for Ripple and there are reasons why they think it would replace current payment and trading   systems.

Fast transactions

Current Bitcoin transactions take around 40 minutes to complete. Ripple transactions happen in a couple of seconds. Ripple works on a system of IOUs and these are transferred instantaneously in the system, so it doesn't depend on the transaction times of any currency it deals with.

Since it doesn't depend on multiple layers of financial institutions like local banks, credit companies, brokers, and money transfer services, which makes payment and trading slow and expensive, it's the simplest and cheapest way to pay and transfer money. It's a stand-alone system that doesn't depend on third-parties, intermediaries, and other middlemen to complete a transaction.

Currency smorgasbords

The distributed foreign exchange feature of Ripple makes forex trading easier than ever. These days, you don't need to go through a broker to purchase and deal with a currency. In its full implementation, Ripple will allow you to purchase a currency and trade it to another on your own. The system will even make the best value matches for you and complete the deal automatically.

The availability of these currencies at your disposal gives you freedom to choose and deal with those that you prefer, even those currencies that are rarely traded. Payments can also benefit from this feature. The automatic exchange means lower conversion fees because of less number of layers compared to traditional forex pathways.

It works with Bitcoin

While most people see Ripple as a rival, the Ripple system might even enhance Bitcoin by riding in its popularity. It is one of the currencies supported by Ripple currently. A lot of major players, like Google and Lightspeed, have also made investments in Ripple.

Conclusion

I hope this short book was able to help you learn more about the basics of Ripple, the different options you have, and how the future looks for this new currency. Now that you have learned the important factors regarding Ripple, you can finally decide if you want to take the plunge, or if you can recommend it to your family and friends.

Plus, a little addition to your knowledge doesn't hurt, right? It's good to know about new innovations because it keeps you in the know and up-to-date in a world where every big city has groups dedicated to learning more about crypto-currencies.

Finally, if you learned anything from this book, please take the time to share your thoughts by sending me a message or even posting a review to Amazon.

Thank you and good luck!

www.ingramcontent.com/pod-product-compliance
Lightning Source LLC
Chambersburg PA
CBHW071002180526
45168CB00003B/1247

* 9 7 8 1 5 0 7 8 7 7 9 1 3 *